Ready Kindergarten!

A month-by-month guide for preparing your child for Kindergarten

By Sharon Foster

with contributions from former and current Georgia Pre-K Teachers
at Bells Ferry Learning Center including

Laura Thompson and Jennifer Kent

ISBN-13: 978-1537263496

ISBN-10: 1537263498

DEDICATION

For Ms. Charlotte, who taught me how to truly appreciate four-year-olds.

And, for all of the children who have attended the Georgia Pre-K Program at Bells Ferry Learning Center; you brightened our days with your smiles.

Ready? Set? Kindergarten!

CONTENTS

Ready? Set? Kindergarten!

ACKNOWLEDGMENTS

I am so grateful that I get to go to work every day with the entire awesome, amazing, rock star staff of Bells Ferry Learning Center. Although the Lead Pre-K Teachers are specifically credited with contributions, the entire crew is critical in the success of any project. Thanks to Kris Murray for encouraging me to become an expert in my field. Thanks to Verna Slade for always inspiring new adventures. And a whole-hearted thanks to Zack, Shelby, Ben, and Natalie, along with my extended family for their unconditional love and support. Love y'all much.

Ready? Set? Kindergarten!

INTRODUCTION

In almost sixteen years of operating a preschool/child care center, I have heard this question repeatedly, "What does my child need to do to get in to Kindergarten?" Well, the answer is quite simple: Be five. That's it. If your child successfully reaches the fifth year of life, your child is eligible to attend Kindergarten. She may not be fully potty-trained (although almost all are); she may not know the difference between red and green or a circle and a square. That is okay! All your child has to do to "get in" to kindergarten is reach her fifth birthday.

Now, having said that, we all want our children to be as prepared for school as possible. Most children do know the difference between red and green before Kindergarten. Most can recognize a circle and a square and many children also recognize much more advanced shapes. Many children show signs of reading readiness and some have even begun to actually read before their first day of school.

Kindergarten classrooms are made up of children with a variety of backgrounds and developmental levels. There are children who have spent the first four years at home without any type of structured classroom-style learning. They may have been taught some things by their parents but may not have learned some social skills such as how to work and play well within a group; how to form a line to go from the classroom to the playground; and how to wait for their turn to speak or play with a particular item. There are also children who have preschool experiences that will help them function well in a classroom setting. They may, or may not, have mastered more cognitive skills than their stay-at-home peers. It completely depends on the stay-at-home parent and on the quality of the preschool experience. An active, attentive, involved stay-at-home parent will have helped their child reach many more milestones than a child care center that is strictly custodial in nature without much thought to lesson planning, teacher-child interactions, and an appropriate environment that is optimized for learning.

Kindergarten teachers are accustomed to receiving children with very diverse backgrounds. The children who cry because it's their first time away from their parents are just as welcome as the children who are accustomed to a group setting and come in with confidence.

So, if all of this is true, why write a book about kindergarten readiness? Because most parents want to do something to help their children be successful in school. And there are a lot of fun things that parents of preschoolers can do that will lay the foundation for learning. There are everyday, simple activities that help children begin to understand mathematic, literary, and scientific concepts. When they are introduced to these concepts in school, learning will come more readily as the child received preschool exposure to them. Even if your child is in a high-quality preschool environment, these activities will give you ideas for things you can do at home to support the learning that is taking place at preschool.

The chapters ahead will provide parents and caregivers with ideas for simple and fun ways to incorporate learning into everyday activities. They are presented in a month-by-month format that is easy to follow. Most of the activities require little to no advance preparation. Most of them cost little to no money. The idea is to give the child preschool experiences that she can expand upon when she reaches Kindergarten. It is not crucial that a child be able to read and write prior to entering Kindergarten. Those are skills that are learned in Kindergarten. The best thing that parents can do is work on pre-reading and pre-writing skills so that the child is quite receptive and ready to learn these skills in Kindergarten.

Children learn best when an activity is meaningful and relevant to them. A child who has grown up in south Florida will struggle to understand concepts that involve snow and snowmen. A child who has never left Iowa probably won't enjoy activities that are beach-themed. Pick and choose from the activities provided in each chapter. Select the ones that you feel will be best-suited to your child's interests. Never be afraid to expand on an activity if your child loves it and leads you in a new direction. Most of all: have fun! Teach your child that learning is a fantastic, never-ending, completely enjoyable process.

Ready? Set? Go!

2 USING THIS GUIDE

This book is broken down by months of the school year – August through May – plus a summer bridge chapter. The activities listed for each month are mostly seasonal in nature. The activities coordinate with holidays, annual events, and weather patterns. In addition, there are activities that are just fun and easy to do with no particular reason for being done during the suggested month.

Here's how to best put this book to use: At the end of each chapter, you will find a blank calendar. Write in the dates for the month. Review the activities for the month and choose the ones you and your child will enjoy doing together. Write them into the calendar so you can keep up with your plans. As you do the activities, note your child's favorites. You can then go ahead in the book and jot them on a calendar in the future so that you can repeat the activity.

After the calendar, there is a page for notes. Use this page to write anything you may need to remember down the road. Perhaps you want to repeat an activity but make some changes – note them. Perhaps you want to repeat an activity months later to see how much your child has developed. Make notes that you can reflect upon down the road. Definitely ask your child her opinions on different activities and be sure she sees you writing the notes. This reinforces that the words we say can be written on paper – crucial knowledge for a child who is developing pre-reading skills.

Some parents will look at these instructions and think, "I didn't plan on writing lesson plans and taking notes!" That's ok. You can successfully use this book without any extra work. Just pick activities and do them with your child. Have fun. Spend time together. You will get every bit as much enjoyment and see just as much development in your child as the parent who chooses to take a more planned approach.

3 AUGUST

Summer is coming to an end and the school year is beginning. This is the time to start preparing your child with more structured days. If you don't already have an established bedtime routine, start one. Do the same things in the same order each evening so your child knows what to expect next. Children respond beautifully to structure, routine, and understanding of what is expected. Whenever possible, give choices. "You can choose between your red pajamas or your blue ones. Which ones would you like to wear?" Preschool children often misbehave because they want to have some control in a situation. Give them choices frequently so that when they don't have a choice, it's easier for them to accept because they know they have opportunities for control in the very near future. Let's get started…

Have your child practice writing her name. Use a variety of media: crayons and construction paper; pencil and notebook paper; pour sugar or salt on a baking sheet and use fingers to write in it.

Sound out each letter in your name, your child's name, and other familiar words and names.

Ask your child about new friends and teachers at preschool.

Cook a simple recipe together and let your child measure the ingredients.

Start a journal. Your child can draw pictures in it and you can write the words she tells you to accompany the picture. Your journal can have a theme or just be filled with random thoughts. Decide how often you will write in it and then schedule times to do it.

Get a Sunday paper and clip coupons for things you typically buy.

Let your child cut out pictures of her favorite foods from grocery store ads and then sort them by food groups.

Using sidewalk chalk, color on your driveway.

Make up an imaginary friend.

Help your child learn how to use a small appliance with your close supervision. (toaster, mixer)

Go to the library together.

Talk with your child about your job. What do you do at work?

Color something green.

Go outside and play in the sprinkler or have a water balloon fight.

Hang a hummingbird feeder outside of your window and watch for hummingbirds to come to it.

Try a new food together.

Play with dough (homemade or store-bought). Use kitchen gadgets to roll, cut and shape the dough.

Build something together with Legos or similar building brick toys. Talk about what you are building. Let your child take the lead role in telling you what to build and how.

Make up a story together. Take turns inventing the next sentence.

On a piece of paper, draw a variety of lines horizontally across the page. Use wavy lines, straight lines, zig-zag lines. Let your child practice cutting along the lines.

Go to a pool and talk about the numbers on the sides of the pool (depths) and what they mean.

Make homemade blocks: save sturdy cardboard boxes such as shoeboxes and boxes from package deliveries. Wrap them with adhesive shelf liner (such as Contact brand) then stack and build.

Search the internet for File Folder games and make some to play with your child. There are lots of free printables out there and you don't have to be an expert crafter to make them.

Plant a fall garden if you live in a warm climate. In the south, we can plant lettuce, broccoli, cabbage, beans, collards, and lots of other fall veggies with time to harvest well into October. If you live in a cooler climate, try an indoor herb garden in a sunny window.

Take a 'back-to-school' picture of your child. Save it for a comparison at the end of the school year.

Let your child help you put groceries away and teach spatial relationships at the same time by saying "Put this next to that. Put this on top of that. Put this under that. Put this on the bottom shelf."

Remember:

It is very important that you read

with your child for 30 minutes every day!

AUGUST

Sun	Mon	Tue	Wed	Thu	Fri	Sat

NOTES

4 SEPTEMBER

For those who didn't return to school in August (like we do in Georgia), now it's back-to-school time! It's a great time to stock up on school supplies for the year as all the stores have super low price sales. Make a list with your child of things she would like to have and shop together. Look through sale ads together for the best prices. Then, move on to these fun activities for September:

Give your child a plastic produce bag at the grocery store and ask her to count out a specific number of a produce item.

While driving, talk about traffic signs and community signs. Ask your child to 'read' signs that are familiar to them (fast food restaurant signs, retail stores they have visited with you, etc.)

Learn a new card game and play it together.

Gather take out menus from your favorite restaurants and play restaurant at home.

Save pits from fresh peaches and germinate them. Buy from a local farmers market so you know the peach variety is good for your climate. There are a number of YouTube videos and online tutorials that explain how to grow a peach tree from a peach pit.

Make a leaf rubbing by putting a leaf under a piece of paper and rubbing over it with crayon.

Get a book you have never read. Ask your child to tell you what she thinks the story is about just by looking at the picture on the cover.

Play in the dirt or in a sandbox. Feel it, measure it, put it through a funnel, pour it from one container to another.

While reading with your child, ask about what's happening in the story and try to predict the ending.

Make an at-home 'dress up box' filled with old clothes, hats, accessories and shoes. Make themed prop boxes, too, for pretending to be a vet, hairstylist, waitress, doctor...anything that interests your child.

Bake cookies and visit the police or fire station in honor of 9/11.

Help your child learn how to blow her nose, wash her hands, wipe her bottom, and brush her hair independently.

Play a different type of music at home, maybe something from another culture, and talk about how it sounds.

Fly at flag at home for Labor Day. Count the number of stars and stripes. Talk about the pattern of the stripes (red, white, red, white)

Make up sentences together using alliteration: Bob's big brother bought baby a bottle. Sally sat sweetly so Susie could swing. The sentences don't even have to make sense – you are just practicing recognition of sounds that are the same. Jose had hard hair on his house.

Build a fort around your dining room table with blankets and pillows.

Save empty toilet paper tubes. When you have enough, make 'people blocks' by taping a picture of each family member onto a tube.

Buy several types of dried beans. Put them in a big pile and then sort them. After you've finished sorting, wash them and make bean soup.

Make up a story about a frog who couldn't jump.

Make musical instruments by putting dried beans or uncooked rice in between two paper plates, then glue or staple the plates together completely around the outer edges. Let your child decorate her instruments.

Ask your child to draw a picture that makes her happy; one that makes her angry; one that makes her sad.

Buy a box of Fruit Loops and make patterns with the colored rings.

Write your child's name on a piece of paper with plenty of space around each letter. Cut a square or rectangle around each letter to make separate pieces. Shuffle them up and let your child practice putting them in the right order to spell her name. At first, you might have to write her name and let her match up the cut pieces to her written name. Eventually, she will be able to do it on her own.

Look for things around your house that are: hard, soft, bumpy, rough, smooth, fuzzy. Make a graph to find out which texture appears most often in your home.

Remember:

It is very important that you read

with your child for 30 minutes every day!

SEPTEMBER

Sun	Mon	Tue	Wed	Thu	Fri	Sat

NOTES

5 OCTOBER

Fall is here! The weather is cooling. Leaves are changing color. There is so much happening in the world around you. Don't let life keep you too busy to watch the changes with your child and talk about them. When my daughter was very young, we were on a walk together once. She said to me, "Mommy, I like walking with Grandma because she lets me stop as long as I want to look at stuff." Such an innocent statement from a young child and a real eye-opener for me! From that moment on, I tried to walk like Grandma and let my little one explore to her heart's content. There's a reason that "stop and smell the roses" is an expression. Don't walk too quickly past the roses.

Bake pumpkin seeds together. Taste them before and after baking and talk about how they taste different.

Buy or make a jump rope. Sing a song while jumping rope.

Go on an 'orange' scavenger hunt. Find orange things inside and outside of the house. Count how many orange items you each collect and find out who has more.

Talk to a grandparent and ask them to tell stories of their youth.

Have a tea party.

Get a magazine or newspaper and cut out every word you find that starts with the letter 'O'.

Practice a family escape plan in case of fire emergency. Draw a plan. Where will each family member go? How will you exit your home? What should you look for on the way out? (heavy smoke, hot doors, etc.)

Go on a nature walk and talk about the leaves changing colors.

Count pinecones or acorns.

Discuss what your child wants to be for Halloween and why. If you don't observe the holiday, talk with your child about your family beliefs and the fact that different cultures and religions observe different holidays.

Write seasonal words (Halloween, bats, pumpkins, fall, orange, leaves, autumn) on paper. Let your child use magnetic letters to match the letters in the words you wrote.

Go to a pumpkin patch and find the biggest pumpkin, the smallest pumpkin. Find ones that are round and ones that are more oval.

Draw a picture using only squares.

Count how many windows are in your house or apartment.

Draw a family tree.

Learn how to play Dominoes.

Get out pots and pans and wooden spoons. Have a marching band.

Let your child create an art project, not a craft, an art project. Crafts are made when the adult chooses the materials and a specific outcome is expected. Art is created when you let your child choose the medium and how to use it with no expectations of the finished product's appearance.

Make a chore chart with your child. Help her choose the items that she can and will help with around the house. Decide on a reward for completion. Avoid material objects or candy as the reward. Instead, choose an experience you can share. A trip to a favorite park, a picnic, a family movie night or game night are a few ideas.

Make up a silly story about a pumpkin who wanted to become a pie.

Ask your child to draw a picture. Then, let her tell you about her picture. You "caption" her picture by writing what she tells you verbatim.

Practice moving cotton balls or pom poms from one container to another using tweezers.

Read the book "Chicka Chicka Boom Boom" by Bill Martin, Jr. and John Archambault.

Trace an outline of your child's body on a big piece of brown craft paper. (Find inexpensive rolls of this type of paper at a paint store.) Let her paint or color her life size self portrait.

Save plastic caps from milk jugs, orange juice containers, and other types of beverages. Use them to make a sorting game, a counting game, or a matching game. (a Pinterest search will give you tons of ideas if you are drawing a blank)

Remember:

It is very important that you read

with your child for 30 minutes every day!

OCTOBER

Sun	Mon	Tue	Wed	Thu	Fri	Sat

NOTES

6 NOVEMBER

November is loaded with events that spark themed activities. Veteran's Day, Election Day, and Thanksgiving all lend themselves to many teachable moments. Include your child in planning the Thanksgiving meal. Pick an old favorite recipe to make together or search Pinterest for a fun, new idea. Even if your Pinterest recipe turns into one of those famous "Pinterest Fails", you have still spent valuable time with your child and that is a win.

Make a sandwich and cut it in half.

Teach your child about random acts of kindness. Perform one together.

Completely silly game: Turkey Bowling! Save 10 water bottles. Set them up like bowling pins. Use a frozen turkey to try and knock down as many bowling pins as possible.

Look in books for community helpers and discuss their jobs with your child. What do they do? Why are they important? How do they help us?

Search for things that are square in your home.

Make a homemade book about pilgrims.

Make a graph—ask each family member what they like on their pizza.

Draw a fall picture.

Choose two different types of apples, such as Granny Smith and Red Delicious. Clean them, cut them, taste them, and let each family member vote for their favorite. Count the ballots and see which apple was elected the family favorite.

Color a picture of something purple.

Plan a meal and cook it together.

Write down your favorite family Thanksgiving tradition.

How many words can you think of that start with N, like November?

Measure things around the house with a tape measure.

Draw a picture using only circles.

Make a list of things for which your family is thankful.

If your family says grace before meals, write your own prayer or learn a new one. Take turns saying a new grace each evening.

Build a campfire and make s'mores.

Let your child choose some toys she has outgrown and donate them to a thrift store, shelter, church, or preschool.

Remember:

It is very important that you read

with your child for 30 minutes every day!

NOVEMBER

Sun	Mon	Tue	Wed	Thu	Fri	Sat

NOTES

7 DECEMBER

This is a month that is just chocked full of themes, ideas, traditions, and super cool activities. If your child is in preschool, she may likely have some time off for the holiday break – a perfect opportunity to spend more time together on simple and fun learning experiences. If your child is at home with you and not in preschool, this is a great time to work on some more in-depth projects together. If you celebrate Christmas with gifts, why not try making some homemade/DIY gifts? Grandparents, especially, treasure these types of keepsakes. In our house, we always made a simple craft for each of our closest neighbors. As my children have grown, the tradition has changed slightly. We spend most of the day on Christmas Eve baking homemade cinnamon rolls. We package them up and deliver them to our neighbors in the afternoon so they have a yummy sweet treat to enjoy on Christmas morning. We use Pioneer Woman/Ree Drummond's recipe. It's fabulous and always turns out just perfectly! The added bonus is the amazing aroma of cinnamon that fills our home.

Look around the house and find items that start with 'S'.

Discuss how the world changes in the winter. Don't forget to discuss why these changes occur.

Cut pictures out of a magazine of things that start with "P".

Talk about how your family celebrates holidays. If you don't celebrate holidays, talk about how and why your beliefs are different from those who do celebrate.

Let your child teach you a new song.

Make a homemade book about a Christmas ornament who didn't have a tree to live on.

Color a picture using only red and green crayons.

Play a board game—Candyland is a great game for beginners.

Count plates, forks, and cups as you set the dinner table together.

Cut pictures out of a magazine of things that are red.

Count the number of people in your family.

Draw a picture together of your family.

Purchase a small (table-top size) artificial tree for your child's bedroom. Make homemade ornaments together to adorn the tree.

Start a collection.

Have a silly discussion about what it would be like if you had an elephant for a pet.

Make a pact that your family will eat dinner together at the table, with no TV, at least three times each week.

Sing the ABC song together.

Cut leftover gift wrapping paper into squares. Make a collage.

Learn about a holiday that you don't typically celebrate in your family.

Go on an evening Christmas Lights tour and find the most spectacularly decorated homes.

Go on a scavenger hunt for words at the mall. Make a list of seasonal words that you will expect to see and then count how many you find. Examples: sale, Christmas, holiday, gift, stocking stuffer, special

Visit an assisted living home and sing Christmas carols with the residents. Make cards to take with you so you can leave a gift. Be sure to call ahead to ask if this is okay and perhaps schedule a good time for them. There may be an activities director who can make arrangements.

Using magnetic plastic numbers (refrigerator magnets), practice putting the numbers in order from left to right. You can do this right on the fridge or use a baking sheet.

Make a marble painting. Line the lid of a shoe box with paper. Dip a few marbles in paint. You can use one color or multiple colors, if you like. Put the paint-covered marbles in the box and tilt the box in different directions so the marbles roll all over, creating your marble painting.

Remember:

It is very important that you read

with your child for 30 minutes every day!

DECEMBER

Sun	Mon	Tue	Wed	Thu	Fri	Sat

NOTES

8 JANUARY

Happy New Year! We are halfway through the school year now and Kindergarten is fast approaching. By now, you've probably realized a common theme to our activities: Quality time spent together with your child. Really – it doesn't matter what you are doing. What's important is that you are doing it together! So, let's move along with fun and simple ideas for the second half of the school year.

Have your child write thank you letters for gifts (children who are unable to write words can draw a picture).

Make a friends and family birthday calendar. Every month, mail homemade birthday cards.

Find shapes in the road signs on the way to school or the store.

Make one New Year's Resolution together. Discuss what you will do differently and why. Plan ways to fulfill your resolution so that it lasts longer than a week or two.

Play 'restaurant' at dinnertime. Let your child make menus for each member of the family to order from, take orders from the menu, and then fix each person's plate according to their order. This will take some parental assistance at first. But, kids love this game and become able to do it independently after some practice.

Look for patterns around your house in different fabrics such as rugs, drapes, clothing, and bedspreads.

Write the alphabet together.

Ask your child to finish the sentence "I have a dream…"

Discuss with your child the history of Martin Luther King and the reason that Martin Luther King Day is a holiday.

Let your child set the table. Make placemats together with outlines that show where each item goes (plate, utensils, napkins, glass).

Watch a TV program with your child and discuss the show.

Have a family game night.

Read Eric Carle's book "Brown Bear, Brown Bear, What Do You See?"

Help your child identify colors and items at the grocery store.

Give your child a handful of change and let him sort it.

Make up a silly song together.

Search the internet for a list of fun and silly holidays you can celebrate together this year. (www.timeanddate.com is one resource) Choose one for each month and create unique celebration ideas.

Find a pen pal and write letters. You could call a preschool in another city or state and ask if their Pre-K class would be interested in having a pen pal.

Buy a bag of trail mix or Chex Mix at the store and sort it. Decide which pile of pieces has the most and the least. You can also use the words 'more' and 'less' in this activity.

Open a book to a random page. Close your eyes and point to a word. How many words can you think of that rhyme with that word?

Count how many things you can find in your house that start with the letter 'P'.

Make scrambled eggs. Talk about how the eggs change during the process.

Pop popcorn and then eat it with a straw bent in half to form tongs.

Learn how to count to five in Spanish.

Remember:

It is very important that you read

with your child for 30 minutes every day!

JANUARY

Sun	Mon	Tue	Wed	Thu	Fri	Sat

NOTES

_____

_____

_____

_____

_____

_____

_____

_____

9 FEBRUARY

Love is in the air! February is most well-known for Valentine's Day but there are a lot of other fun events this month. Mardi Gras, Chinese New Year, National Children's Dental Health Month, and President's Day just to name a few. Let's explore some of the opportunities February has to offer.

Watch the Super Bowl and talk with your child about teamwork.

Black History Month—discuss famous African-Americans.

Discuss why people celebrate Mardi Gras. Make or buy a King Cake. What colors are associated with Mardi Gras?

Have Chinese food for dinner on Chinese New Year. Let your child choose whether you go to a restaurant, pick up take out, get delivery, or make your own.

Cut the bottom off of a stalk of celery. Put the celery stalk in a glass of water with food coloring in it. Watch the celery stalk change color as it draws in the colored water.

Have a family movie night—pop popcorn together. Not a microwave bag...real on-the-stovetop popcorn. Talk about the difference in the popcorn before and after it's cooked.

Find out what things begin with 'X'.

Help your child sign Valentine cards.

Talk about Abraham Lincoln and George Washington on their birthdays.

On President's Day, talk about the duties of America's President.

Ask your child to tell you what she would do if she were President.

Practice writing your child's name together

Discussion question: Why are teeth important?

Sort the things in your pantry according to which foods are good for teeth and which foods are bad for teeth.

Let your child tell you a bedtime story.

If you are in a snowy area, go sledding or build a snowman. If you aren't, talk about snow. Search the internet together for pictures of snowy places. Find a recipe for homemade fake snow using baking soda and try making it together.

Make homemade Valentine's Day cards and mail them to far away family members.

Plan a summer vacation.

Paint with things other than a paintbrush. Try a sponge, a plastic fork and spoon, fingers, an old toothbrush, or even a tennis ball.

Remember:

It is very important that you read

with your child for 30 minutes every day!

FEBRUARY

Sun	Mon	Tue	Wed	Thu	Fri	Sat

NOTES

10 MARCH

In Atlanta, where I live, the weather in March is incredibly unpredictable. We have had blizzards in early March and then enjoyed beautiful sunshine and warmth a couple of short weeks later. No matter where you are, it's a good idea to have plenty of indoor and outdoor ideas for March because you never know what this month will bring.

Pick out healthy foods together at the grocery store.

Make homemade recycled crayons together. Gather small old pieces of crayon. Remove any paper. Put the pieces in a lightly greased muffin tin. (You can also use a silicon muffin pan and skip the grease.) Bake for 15 minutes at 250 degrees. Cool and remove from tin. Now you have multicolored circular crayons that will make really cool multicolor drawings.

Write a poem. It doesn't have to make sense, just make it rhyme.

Read your favorite Dr. Seuss book together on March 2 (Dr. Seuss' birthday). Bake a cake together and have a birthday party.

Fly a kite.

Go to www.q4kidz.org to sign up to receive daily whimsical and conversation-starting questions by text. Enjoy the interesting answers your child will give.

Put green food coloring in your milk on St. Patrick's Day.

Sort a deck of cards by suit. Shuffle and sort again by numbers.

Learn a line dance together.

Study the night sky and find Uranus (discovered on March 13, 1781.)

Watch the weather on TV one night. The next day, discuss whether the forecast was correct.

Look around and name all of the green things you can find.

Find Ireland on a map.

Admire the artwork of Vincent Van Gogh.

Discussion question: What is Mount Rushmore and where is it?

Talk about Albert Einstein on his birthday (March 14).

Make green gelatin and talk about how it changes from liquid to solid when it's refrigerated.

Listen to music by Johann Sebastian Bach on his birthday (March 21).

Cut out pictures from a magazine of things that start with 'H'.

Do jumping jacks to your favorite song.

Ask your child to teach you a favorite song learned at school, church, or from friends.

Pick one food that no one in your family has ever eaten. Try it together.

Make up a story about a leprechaun who lost his pot of gold.

Search the internet for 'preschool science experiments'. Pick one and conduct the experiment together. Remember that predicting the outcome is an important part of science experiments.

Go to your favorite places around your neighborhood or community and take selfies together. Print the pictures and make a photo album.

Pick some type of living thing that your child can help care for. If your family prefers not to have pets, try a plant.

April Fool's Day is coming. Plan a harmless fun prank to play on a family member, friend, or neighbor.

Get a seed starter kit and plant seeds indoors so the seedlings are ready to be planted outside after the last frost.

Let your child help with laundry. She can sort dirty clothes by lights, darks, colors. She can sort clean clothes by owner, match socks, and begin to learn how to fold.

Pretend you are a tourist in your own town. Where would you go? What sights would you see? Plan a whole weekend of 'staycation' adventures.

Fill a baking sheet that has edges, like a jelly roll pan, with salt or sugar. Use your fingers to draw and write in it.

Make your own puzzle. Print an 8 x 10 of a favorite photo. Glue it to cardboard and decoupage the top. Turn it over and draw puzzle pieces on the back. Cut them out and build your puzzle.

Teach your child how to make her own bed.

Remember:

It is very important that you read

with your child for 30 minutes every day!

MARCH

Sun	Mon	Tue	Wed	Thu	Fri	Sat

NOTES

11 APRIL

The arrival of spring makes me happy! Partially because I love summer and spring means summer is drawing near. But I also love watching the world come back to life. The leaves appearing on trees, blossoms popping up on Dogwood trees, more birds singing in the backyard, the bright yellow forsythia blooming outside my kitchen window. If I'm being honest, the forsythia actually sits in my neighbor's yard. I love them for resisting their urge to cut it down because they know how much joy it brings to me. Remember the story in the October chapter about stopping to smell the roses? April is an excellent time for long walks and nature watching. Enjoy!

Keep a weather chart for the month.

Discuss where you would go for spring break if you could travel anywhere in the world.

Look at the newspaper together.

Talk a nature walk together on Earth Day (April 22).

Make a list of words that start with 'A' like 'April'.

Dance to your favorite songs.

Make up a silly story about a dog that can talk.

Watch TV together and talk about the commercials that you see.

Walk around like different animals; be a duck, a frog, a rabbit, a horse, an elephant, a crab.

Discussion question: What did Paul Revere do on April 18, 1775?

Cut pictures out of a magazine of things that start with the letter 'T'.

Have a family board game night. Connect 4 is a great preschool game for building math skills.

Read a Hans Christian Anderson story in honor of his birthday (April 2, 1805).

Let your child choose an entire menu for dinner, using all food groups, and help you cook it.

George Washington became our first President on April 30, 1789. How many Presidents have we had since?

Buy some individual cardboard cartons of milk or juice (like the ones they serve at elementary schools). Help your child practice opening them. I was once told by a group of Kindergarten teachers that this was the number one skill they wished we would teach in Pre-K.

Go outside and practice skipping, jumping, and hopping on one foot.

Draw rainbows. Name the colors.

Go outside and look for four-leaf clovers.

Buy a butterfly kit and watch caterpillars transform.

If your town has safe and reliable public transportation, take a ride on it. You don't even have to have a specific destination in mind. Just look out the window and talk about the places you see.

Invite some friends over and play Duck, Duck, Goose.

Teach your child her phone number and address very easily by singing it to the tune of any song you like. You'd be surprised at how fast children learn something by singing it versus simply speaking the words.

Tell your child about your favorite childhood memory.

Make dirt pudding. Put chocolate pudding in a bowl, cover it with chocolate sandwich cookies (such as Oreos) that have been crumbled into fine pieces, stick a few gummy worms into your dirt. Enjoy!

Make shakers with empty water bottles. Fill them about half way with rice or beans. Decorate them with pretty ribbons tied around the necks. Dance around to your favorite song with your shaker bottles.

Search your house for things that start with the same letter as your child's first name.

Remember:

It is very important that you read

with your child for 30 minutes every day!

APRIL

Sun	Mon	Tue	Wed	Thu	Fri	Sat

NOTES

_____

_____

_____

_____

_____

_____

_____

_____

12 MAY

The school year is winding down. Spring fever is in the air. Days are getting longer and summer is just around the corner. Think back on the beginning of the school year. What skills have you seen your child develop during this year? What new discoveries have you made together? What skills do you think your child still needs to improve upon? What activities can you do to encourage development in that area?

Make a Mexican meal together on Cinco de Mayo (May 5th). Make mariachis by putting rice in a plastic Easter egg and taping two plastic spoons on either side of the egg.

Draw a picture of all the 'Moms' in your family including grandmothers, aunts, etc.

Plant your garden from the seedlings you started in March.

Watch the Kentucky Derby together, read the names of all the horses, and imagine your own horse's name.

Make homemade pizza.

Frank Baum's birthday is May 15, 1856. What famous story did he write?

Let your child tell you a bedtime story.

Spread peanut butter on a pinecone, roll it in birdseed, and hang it from a tree outside. Watch birds that come to feed from it.

Make up a silly song about flowers that refuse to grow. Sing it to the tune of London Bridges.

Tell your child about your favorite childhood book. Read it together if you have it.

Take a trip to the library. Sign up for a library card if you don't have one already.

Look at a map together and find places such as home, school, friends and family member's houses, your favorite places to shop, grocery stores, parks, restaurants.

Practice writing numbers.

Go outside and make movement patterns together. (ex: hop, hop, jump, jump, twirl, twirl, hop, hop)

Make a picnic together and go to a park to eat it.

Reflect on all the activities you've done together from this book. Decide on your favorites and do them again.

Go to the zoo.

Invent your own board game.

On a pretty spring day, take a long drive together. Play your favorite songs and sing as loud as you can.

Go on an 'M' hunt around your home. Find as many things as you can that start with 'M' like May.

Go to the nearest airport and watch planes take off and land. Discussion topics are endless: the science of flight, travel topics, making up stories about where the people are from on the planes that are landing.

Plan a 'last day of school' party. Who will you invite? What will you eat? What games will you play?

Make mud pies.

Go to a pottery studio and paint ceramics.

Draw a hopscotch board on your driveway with sidewalk chalk and play hopscotch together.

Teach your child how to play the card game War.

Pick wildflowers and make a bouquet for your home.

Play catch.

Make a Diet Coke and Mentos geyser. If you've never heard of it, a Google search will provide instructions and videos. It is really fun and definitely an OUTDOORS activity!

Take a picture of your child and compare to the picture you took last August. Ask her how she has changed.

Remember:

It is very important that you read

with your child for 30 minutes every day!

MAY

Sun	Mon	Tue	Wed	Thu	Fri	Sat

NOTES

13 SUMMER

Oh, how I love summer! I thoroughly enjoy being outdoors, living life at a slower pace, and the long days with sunshine well into the evening. I would add cooking dinner on the grill to that list, but I live in the south where grilling is basically a year-round activity. I am a believer that children should have the chance to be children in the summer. I do understand the concept of summer learning loss. At this young age, however, I think that the best learning takes place through everyday play and activities.

Most of all, learning takes place when parents spend time with their children. Have meaningful conversations together. Ask open-ended questions (those with more than a 'yes' or 'no' answer and those that have no right or wrong answer). When your child brings you a piece of artwork she has created, avoid the urge to say "Oh! I love that!". By saying this, she learns that her work has to be validated and requires adult approval. Instead, try saying "Wow! Tell me about your work. How did you make that? What do you like the best about it?" That will teach your child that her opinion of the quality of her work is important. It will instill in her a confidence to create, try new things, and enjoy her successes based on her own approval.

If you decide to relax routines and rules a little bit over the summer, just remember to get back into a structured routine a few weeks before school starts. Your child will not understand that she was allowed to go to bed at 10:00 pm all summer and then has to go to bed at 8:00 pm all of a sudden on the night before school starts.

One thing I would not relax about over the summer is reading. I've already written it ten times in this book so I might as well write it one last time. **Remember: It is very important that you read with your child for 30 minutes every day!** Why do I keep hammering this point? It is the single most important thing you can do to insure your child's future academic success. Numerous studies have shown that children who are read to by their parents or caregivers have better language skills than their peers; are more likely to read on level or above level by third grade; and are more likely to graduate from high school. Don't miss this opportunity to spend time with your child, give her your undivided attention, and set the wheels in motion for future success.

Now, you are ready for Kindergarten!

NOTES

NOTES

_____

_____

_____

_____

_____

_____

_____

_____

ABOUT THE AUTHOR

Sharon Foster is the owner of two successful child care centers in Woodstock and Marietta, Georgia. (Bells Ferry Learning Centers). She holds a TCD in Early Childhood Education as well as a National Administrators Credential. Sharon began working in child care at the young age of 13 in 1978. She worked after school and full-time during the summers until 1983. Sharon went on to spend many years in the hospitality industry, but always with the dream of getting back into the child care business. Her dream came true in 2001 when she purchased her first center. In spring, 2016 she opened her second location and is enjoying watching it grow.

Sharon loves building relationships with families in the community and takes her responsibilities very seriously. She knows people are trusting her with their most precious treasures!

Sharon has been married to Zack for more than 22 years and they have three children, Shelby, Ben, and Natalie. She is an avid runner and her other hobbies include watching Georgia Tech football and going to concerts—especially Zac Brown Band concerts!

Check out the following links for more information…
www.BellsFerryLC.com
www.facebook.com/bellsferrylc
www.facebook.com/BFLCMarietta

Contributing authors Jennifer Kent and Laura Thompson have been teaching Georgia's Pre-K program at Bells Ferry Learning Center for many years. Both are certified through the Georgia Professional Standards Commission and are graduates of Kennesaw State University.

Made in the USA
Monee, IL
20 March 2021